EXPLORING THEATER

Choreography and Dance in Theater

Don Rauf

Cavendish
Square

New York

Published in 2018 by Cavendish Square Publishing, LLC
243 5th Avenue, Suite 136, New York, NY 10016

Library of Congress Cataloging-in-Publication Data

Names: Rauf, Don.
Title: Choreography and dance in theater / Don Rauf.
Description: New York . Cavendish Square, 2018. | Series: Exploring theater | Includes index.
Identifiers: ISBN 9781502630018 (library bound) | ISBN 9781502630025 (ebook)
| ISBN 9781502634283 (paperback)
Subjects: LCSH: Dance--Juvenile literature. | Choreography--Juvenile literature. | Theater--
Production and direction--Juvenile literature.
Classification: LCC GV1596.5 R38 2018 | DDC 792.78--dc23

Editorial Director: David McNamara
Editor: Fletcher Doyle
Copy Editor: Nathan Heidelberger
Associate Art Director: Amy Greenan
Designer: Jessica Nevins
Production Coordinator: Karol Szymczuk
Photo Research: J8 Media

CONTENTS

Ballet provides the technique, strength, and discipline needed for all forms of dance.

CHAPTER ONE

So You Think You Can Dance?

Sebastian Mesler, an eighteen-year-old from Seattle, started dancing when he was four years old. He tried soccer and other after-school activities, but dance was something he always enjoyed more than anything else. When he entered the men's division at Pacific Northwest Ballet at age thirteen, every day after school was dedicated to lessons and rehearsals. Through middle school and high school, he would dance for fourteen hours each week spread out over six days, and have one day completely off to give his body some rest.

During his intensive summer classes, Mesler spent entire days—about thirty hours a week—dedicated to dance. Outside of class, he put time into building his strength and flexibility. "A lot of time was spent keeping your body from breaking, and that entailed stretching and your own personal physical therapy," he says. "You had to dedicate many hours outside of class just to build upper body strength, make sure your core was strong, and your knees weren't going to blow out."

Not everyone interested in dancing in theater has to go into it with the intensity shown by Sebastian

Mesler. Musical theater productions put on by high schools and community groups often give young people a chance to see what dancing in the theater is all about. From these opportunities, a student may get some idea of what it takes to be a professional dancer and/or choreographer. These artists may have the most physically demanding jobs in the theater world. And if dancing isn't for you, the world of theater offers a range of opportunities—both on and off stage—for every type of student, from those who will pursue it as a serious career to those who just want to give it a try.

Putting Your Body to the Test

Those who complain about being on their feet don't know what it's like to be a dancer. Many professional dance performances require three to eight hours of rehearsal daily. A 2017 *New York Times* article described twenty-four-year-old Claire Kretzschmar's grueling schedule in the corps de ballet of the New York City Ballet. Along with the possible seven performances a week, it was typical for the young dancer to have company class each morning, followed by back-to-back-to-back rehearsals. She had occasional breaks for costume fittings or physical therapy, then a pause to have her hair and makeup readied for daily performances. Many nights after her performance, she wound up at home in front of the TV with her feet in an ice bucket.

While the work life of a corps de ballet member may be particularly grueling, most dancers in any professional theater show have exhausting schedules.

A dancer's feet can take a pounding from hours of rehearsing and performing on hard surfaces.

Even if no performances are upcoming, dancers and choreographers must maintain their most important tool: their body.

For any high school student considering a life in dance, the first question may be, "Am I ready to dedicate myself to the full physicality demanded by this field?" Mesler's schedule shows just how intensive training for life as a dancer can be—there's often little time for anything else.

Because a dancer's body is his or her instrument, the young artist must dedicate energy to maintaining it. The College Board recommends learning about good nutrition, **cross-training**, and other ways of taking care of your body. As with an athlete, the career path is a rigorous one, and the body will undergo a lot of wear and tear. Those heading down this path should know that many dancers stop performing by the time they are in their later thirties because it becomes physically too hard to do. Then they may move on to another career, either related to dance or something else entirely.

The Pros Start Young

Most young people who seriously pursue dance know from an early age that they enjoy movement and being physical. Most likely, they have a certain amount of athleticism. And they understand that, just as with sports, dance requires dedication and practice to become good at the craft.

In an article in *Backstage*, Lisa Jo Sagolla, a New York choreographer and dance/theater critic, writes that reaching a professional level in dance requires years of study, so "aspiring dancers must begin training at a very young age."

It helps to develop technique early on. Then dance movement comes more easily as part of muscle memory. Once dancers have these techniques ingrained, they develop their craft even further. Many who pursue this art form start training as young children in dance studios, private classes, and academies. As young as age three, a child might take a creative movement class. Activities like skipping, jumping, and hopping can introduce children to concepts of time and movement. Making motions to music is a great place to start.

Michael Kerr, a dance teacher at New Voices School of Academic & Creative Arts in Brooklyn, introduces his sixth grade students to the idea of body parts, body shapes, and body actions. "They look at the types of body shapes that they can make with the human body—it's either curvy, straight, angular, or a combination of the two or three," he says. "And then I have them work in pairs. They decide visually how they want to create shapes in unison or in contrast to each other. You have decision-making going on. That becomes the basis for thinking independently but in relation to others. Once they work in duets, then I put them in trios or quartets— it's a building-block collaboration."

Lessons like this show students not only the very basics of moving a body to music but also how to explore creating their own dance moves. Those interested in choreography— or actually composing their own dance movements and bringing them to life— need to master the basics of dance. To become good at any art, artists need to master the tools and then aggressively pursue chances to create their own works.

Ballet as a Building Block

Many students who are serious about dance take ballet classes because this art form is at the foundation of many different dance styles and techniques, including those used in Broadway musicals. For example, the "Bottle Dance" in the musical *Fiddler on the Roof*, in which dancers balance bottles on their heads, combines the precision of ballet with the energy of klezmer (traditional eastern European Jewish music). Typically, students learn ballet through group and individual lessons. Through ballet, Sebastian Mesler learned the value of partnering. Many numbers in musical theater feature a male and a female partner. Partnering has been a favorite part of dance for Mesler. He enjoys acquiring a sense of

Ballet influences many musical numbers, including the "Bottle Dance" from *Fiddler on the Roof.*

how to work in fluid unison with another person. "You become good friends with your partners—most of the time," Mesler says. "There's a lot of trust." He has had to throw, catch, lift, and support partners in many productions.

Mastering dance often requires attending private dance studios or hiring a private dance coach who can work on individual needs. If that's out of your economic range, community groups often offer lessons for dance groups. A YMCA or YWCA may have affordable classes. Most of the time, dance is a collaborative effort, so those starting out should take advantage of all opportunities to dance with others.

Try as Much as Possible

Getting involved in any dance production helps with networking. As with most professional fields, success is often tied to whom you know. Making more connections builds a personal network that can lead to opportunity.

Like any career in the arts, the dance and choreography field is fiercely competitive, so fledgling hoofers need to get as much experience and recognition as possible. They also should expect to weather a lot of rejection—getting accustomed to rejection at an early age will only help later on. The actress Angela Cartwright once said, "Rejection is a big part of show business. It can be tough on anyone who doesn't have fairly good self-esteem. Especially kids who are trying to discover who they are." National conventions and competitions provide dancers with a chance to gain awards and evaluate themselves against other young people who are trying to get into the field.

For Sebastian Mesler, part of proving himself and competing meant attending summer programs, workshops, and camps dedicated to dance. For three summers, he attended a summer intensive program in Grand Rapids, Michigan. He did a similar course of study in Austin, Texas, one summer. These classes gave him a chance to broaden his technique, compare himself to other dancers, and further develop himself as a performer.

"In Austin I learned contemporary, jazz, and hip-hop," says Mesler. "I had the opportunity to travel to another city, and I stayed there six weeks in the dorm. I have good friends that I talk with to this day because of it."

Learning different forms of dance early on can help you discover styles at which you excel or that you prefer. The College Board recommends that, to make their high school years count, up-and-coming dancers should practice at least two different types of dance, such as ballet and modern. Branching out makes a person a more desirable dancer to hire.

School Musicals Have Room for All

For most students, school theater productions offer the most and best opportunities to train and perform. These shows give students a chance to see what it's like to prepare for and stage a live performance. Many high schools and some middle schools put on annual productions that let young people go through the entire performance process, including **auditioning**, practicing, collaborating with other actors, and performing live in front of an audience. If your school doesn't offer a program, look into community theater productions. Musicals are not only ideal for perfecting dance moves, they also give performers a chance to sing and act. Dancers who have all these talents (dancing, singing, and acting) may find more work, but it can be hard to master them all. "It's a challenge to get kids to sing and move together at the same time," says Michael Kerr. "Like patting your stomach and tapping your head."

Not everyone is cut out to be a performer, but musicals offer roles for students no matter what their abilities are. Those who really enjoy arts and crafts may create sets, props, and costumes. Technically inclined individuals may participate in the audio engineering and lighting aspects of theater. A people person may be good in the front of the house selling tickets. No matter what your strength or interests, a

theatrical show offers opportunities for all, and each
role is vital.

Push Your Luck

Dancers should always keep an eye out for chances
to perform. A look through Craigslist ads online may
reveal that a local musician is searching for dancers
for his music video. A local amusement park may be
hunting for dance troupe participants to entertain
customers. Sometimes thinking outside the box can
lead to just the right experience. Always be willing to
take a chance. Lucky breaks often come to those who
are looking for them.

Even as a young person, keep a careful record
of all your performance experiences to build a
professional résumé. A résumé that shows dedication,

Young people pursuing dance as
a career should search out any
opportunity to perform.

prolific work, and a range of performances can be the key to paving the way to an audition. Make sure to videotape performances as well. Watching yourself helps improve a performance, and the filmed record may convince those who do the hiring to give you the job.

Watch and Learn

Beyond actually dancing the dance, beginners can learn a lot from observing as well. By attending professional dance performances and musicals and watching them with a critical eye, students can gain an appreciation for dance and an understanding of what contributes to a powerful performance. Go to musicals, dance competitions, ethnic dance performances, and any other live demonstrations. Can't make it out of the house? Watch a performance on your home screen instead. Take out dance movies and musicals from the library, and view performances on YouTube. Dance seems to be more popular than ever, with TV shows such as *Dancing with the Stars*, *World of Dance* with Jennifer Lopez, *Dance Academy*, and *Dance Moms*. Plenty of movies feature dance, but in recent years, films such as *La La Land* have highlighted dancers.

Like many other artists, would-be dancers and choreographers often keep a notebook to jot down sources of inspiration, thoughts on dance moves, and impressions of performances they've seen. As they keep a critical eye trained on dance presentations, they note what they like and dislike. What makes a dance work, or why does it flop?

Advanced Education

After high school, the serious candidates often go on to study at dance schools that have connections with specific dance companies. Many colleges and universities provide bachelor's and/or master's degrees in dance, typically through departments of theater or fine arts. The National Association of Schools of Dance lists about eighty-five accredited dance programs. Students taking these programs delve deeper into coursework in a variety of dance styles, including modern, jazz, ballet, and hip-hop. Skidmore College's dance department stresses technical training in ballet and modern dance. Juilliard in New York City focuses on contemporary dance. Oberlin College and **Conservatory** is dedicated to producing well-rounded dancers. University of California at Berkeley underscores dance as a means of creative expression. Among the other educational institutions that have highly regarded dance programs are Towson University, University of North Carolina, Butler University, Point Park University, Indiana University, the Ailey School, and New York University. A college degree in dance certainly sets a person apart from the competition and can help anyone who wants to pursue dance or choreography as a career.

Most musicals feature ensembles, such as the chimney sweeps dancing to the song "Step in Time" in *Mary Poppins*.

CHAPTER TWO

Teamwork Takes Center Stage

When watching a musical, audience members are often wowed by a magnificent solo performance. While a singular performance can have a great impact, the true magic of a musical production lies in the teamwork involved. Musicals and other theatrical productions depend on the coordinated efforts of many specialists—lighting technicians, stagehands, sound experts, makeup artists, prop designers, costumers, front-of-the-house help, marketers, producers, administrators, musicians, and of course, the performers who deliver the entertainment. Teamwork is the essential ingredient to all great theatrical productions. By getting involved in musical theater, you can see how inspiring it is when people come together to achieve a common goal.

Being able to chip in as an effective team player and understand the power of teamwork translates to any career. DougsGuides.com, a website dedicated to "everything you need to make the transition from college to the real world," features an article "Everything I Needed to Know About Teamwork, I Learned in High School Theatre." The title says it all.

Brian Uzzi, a sociology professor at Northwestern University in Evanston, Illinois, uses the Broadway musical as an example of teamwork at its finest. In an article by Jonah Lehrer in the *New Yorker*, Uzzi says, "Nobody creates a musical by themselves. [It] requires too many different kinds of talent."

Teamwork is especially evident among the dancers in a production. Big dance numbers are the hallmark of the stage musical. In *Beauty and the Beast*, the ensemble of dancers comes together to portray the enchanted household items in the Beast's castle—singing and dancing their way through the song "Be Our Guest." In the musical *Anything Goes*, the stage comes alive in a rousing number that features tap-dancing sailors who are soon joined by tap-dancing women in sunhats. In the musical *Mary Poppins*, the rooftops swarm with gleeful chimney sweeps who bring the stage alive as they twirl their brooms in a massive dance piece. The musical version of *The Producers* has an over-the-top kick line that is part of the epic ensemble dancing during the song "Springtime for Hitler in Germany." Almost every major musical in history has one or more showstopping numbers like these. They are designed to raise audience emotions to a fevered climax, and they all show the power of teamwork among the dancers.

Working Closely with Others

"Teamwork is hugely important in dance," says Brenna Monroe-Cook, who dances professionally with the Limón Dance Company in New York City.

"Moving with other people requires a certain level of trust. And that trust is only possible when everyone is working with attention to each other. That can be very palpable if you're doing partnering with someone. You have to carry their weight or they have to carry yours. You have to counterbalance each other or be in contact in some way. Even when not in contact, we think how we can work to fill the space in the same way or feel the music in the same way."

Monroe-Cook says that teamwork among dancers depends on strong verbal and nonverbal communication. "I might say I'm thinking about this being an angular movement rather than a curving movement," she says. "Sometimes dance communication happens in a nonverbal way in which you are sensing the other person and attending to them and listening to them. It's really teamwork—a building of trust and camaraderie and empathy."

Performing with a partner requires intense collaboration and a willingness to interact in a very physical way with another person.

Each Role for the Greater Whole

A successful production depends on a sense of selflessness from the entire team involved. The directors leading a show, the performers, and the behind-the-scenes crew must know their parts. Dancers, singers, and actors understand when to step back and let the spotlight shine on other cast members.

In the area of dance, the teamwork might begin with the choreographer and the director discussing the production. The choreographer directs and plans the dance moves for actors, so his or her input early on is essential for the whole vision of the production.

A producer may join in on this planning as well. This person can be the lead guiding force or unifying figure in many productions. He or she helps organize the entire effort and may book the theater, raise money, set the budget, and bring together key staff. The producer may hire the creative roles—director and/or music director, set designer, lighting designer, costume designer, choreographer—as well as stage managers, technicians, and stagehands who run the show. The producer is usually the ultimate problem solver and decider. He or she makes sure the production is moving ahead as planned and with all the proper components in place.

The director and/or a music director works closely with the choreographer so that songs, music, and dancing can come together seamlessly.

The producer, director, music director, and choreographer head up the team that decides on the cast. While music directors weigh in on vocal talent,

BEST WORST THING ...

One of the best documentaries about the world of auditioning and performing in a Broadway musical is *Best Worst Thing That Ever Could Have Happened.* The movie tells the story of Stephen Sondheim's *Merrily We Roll Along* from 1981. The musical starred a cast of young actors, ages sixteen to twenty-five. Among them were Jason Alexander, who went on to do *Seinfeld*; Giancarlo Esposito of *Breaking Bad*; and the director of this film, Lonny Price. The young actors portrayed characters who start as adults but get younger as the story moves back in time to the point when they are just starting out in life as young adults.

Sondheim had nothing but hits up until this show. It closed after only sixteen performances. The movie captures the audition process, the thrill of winning a role, the work that goes into a musical, and the disappointment that can occur when a show flops. It also reveals what happened to the performers who starred in the production. It is must-see viewing for any young person who might be considering a career in musical theater.

Director Lonny Price discusses his documentary *Best Worst Thing That Ever Could Have Happened.*

choreographers evaluate dance abilities. An audition to evaluate dancers may be separate from auditions to choose actors and singers. In a school production, choreographers may not expect a vast range of dance talent from the performers. In casting a show, it's often more important for an actor to have positive energy and a basic ability to move to the beat.

Sometimes, however, a musical will demand a higher level of sophistication and very specific dance talents, such as tap dancing or ballet. In the musical *The Lion King*, the performer who takes on the role of Simba must convincingly move with the strength and grace of the lion he portrays. Sometimes the choreography can be almost gymnastic—in one production of *Kiss Me, Kate*, the lead male had to effortlessly scale a three-story balcony to woo his love.

When dancers/performers are selected, they begin intensive collaborative work in perfecting their motions to meet the vision of the choreographer and director and **sync** their movements smoothly with the music. Hours of togetherness and repetition are required to make the result look polished and free from strain. Along the way, as rehearsals progress, the director will be making sure that the dancers are supporting the overall dramatic flow of the script.

The Team Beyond the Stage

In addition to the performers who will fill the stage during the live performance, dancers also coordinate with the other workers who are not in the spotlight. Brenna Monroe-Cook has danced in many productions where lighting, costumes, sets, audio, and makeup are key to heightening the entire experience for the audience. She recently performed a piece in which the lighting was essential for setting the mood, but she felt like she was performing to the Bruce Springsteen song "Dancing in the Dark." The lighting was very dim, which made it difficult to see and dance. "Your visual system is so important in terms of regulating your balance," she says. "It was hard to stand up on that darkened stage. It was hard to stand on one leg or hard to move very slowly in a controlled way because my visual system was messed up."

At first, she and the other dancers in this piece complained about the dim lighting, but then she watched her other cast members from the seats in the audience. She was amazed at what she saw.

"The lights looked stunning," Monroe-Cook says. "The light technician was creating this incredible atmosphere that served the piece so well. In an instance like this, there's a humbling that happens. In theater, you have to see the larger picture and see how all of the players come together to create an experience for the audience. It's easy to get singularly focused on ourselves and our own experience. My experience with the lighting was a good reminder of what collaboration in the theater really is."

She adds that the lighting technicians had to work closely with the music director and sound technician as well because the lights were programmed to respond and change according to shifts in the prerecorded music and the dancers' movements.

Dancers and choreographers often consult with sound technicians. In the Broadway musical *Billy*

Elliot, a large group of young performers tap dance. The sound designer, Paul Arditti, had to figure out how to mix the sound in the theater to perfectly mesh the thunderous tap dancing with the music from the orchestra—one element could not overwhelm the other. The actor who portrayed Billy not only wore two wireless mics to pick up his vocals, he also slipped into a specially equipped pair of track pants before his big tap number. This garment featured a sewn-in wireless pack with two mics—one running down each leg of his pants. The mics amplified his tap sounds, which were essential for this dance piece. Working out these technical issues demanded cooperation between the hoofers and the technical professionals behind the scenes.

Placing microphones requires that stagehands play their role as well. In *Billy Elliot,* these professionals assured that the lead actor's mics were properly attached, and they helped test all the gear before the curtain rose at show time. The voice and the tap shoes had to be coming through the sound system clearly and heard throughout the house.

Other Contributing Artists

Just as with sound, hair and makeup enhances the live entertainment as well. These elements define the characters. Think of one of the most popular musicals of all time—*Cats.* The fifteen dancers not only execute specific catlike dance moves as they assemble for their annual junkyard ball, they also sport detailed makeup that makes them appear to be felines. Their looks involve long whiskers, glitter, face paint, false eyelashes, and big wigs. The show would not exist without the hair and makeup done correctly. (To learn more about this aspect of theater, read the volume in this series titled *Hair and Makeup in Theater*.)

In a similar vein, dancers must be in coordination with prop masters. *Singin' in the Rain* features a group that dances with umbrellas. In *Avenue Q*, the human actors sing, dance, and interact with puppets. The puppets have to be maintained and ready to perform at every curtain rise. (To learn more about this aspect of theater, read the volume in this series titled *Puppetry in Theater*.)

Dancers keenly tune in to all instructions from the stage manager. These professionals organize and coordinate the entire theatrical production. They are typically a communication link among all personnel, so instructions from stage managers must be closely heeded, and if a dancer has any suggestions or concerns, he or she would most likely address them with the stage manager.

Michael Kerr, the dance teacher at the New Voices school in Brooklyn, underscores that communication is key among all the participants in a musical. He has helped mount productions of *Annie, Guys and Dolls, Pirates of Penzance, Grease,* and *Anything Goes*, to name a few. He once confronted an issue about furniture and props on the stage. The tech crew had reconfigured the arrangement of furniture on the stage, but Kerr wasn't informed until about a week before performances were to begin, when he was bringing the cast on the stage to run through one of the dance numbers. He had to discuss the problem with the tech

The dancers in the musical *Cats* show how costumes, makeup, and hair styling contribute to their characters.

crew and rework the dancing with his students to make the performance work.

"Sometimes a miscommunication or oversight happens, and it leads to a compromise," he says. "I had to look at the reality of re-choreographing something and asking students to do something that is quite a challenge for them. In the end, though, the kids always came through."

In an interview for this Exploring Theater series, Greg Kotis recommended that all young people try getting involved in a theater production because it can teach focus, courage, communication, public speaking, patience, and an appreciation for others. Kotis should know. He wrote the story and cowrote the lyrics for the hit musical *Urinetown*. He won a Tony Award for his book (the story/script) and the original score. The characters of Bobby Strong and Hope Cladwell from *Urinetown* were included on *New York Theatre Monthly*'s list of "The 100 Greatest Roles in Musical Theatre." After opening in 2001, the musical had a successful run on Broadway (965 performances), and it has lived on in many regional and school productions.

Kotis, who started doing theater as a sophomore in high school, said, "Being part of a play or musical is a great way of exploring what you can do, how you relate to others, and you make a few friends along the way."

Zac Efron, with Vanessa Hudgens, knew he wanted to dance at a young age.

CHAPTER THREE

Bringing a Production to Life

Zac Efron says that when he was twelve years old, he was geeky, gap-toothed, and liked musicals more than girls. Growing up in Arroyo Grande, California, Efron had few friends, and instead of hanging out in the mall or playing video games, he watched musicals and auditioned and acted in community theater. He pushed himself to audition and performed in *Gypsy* and *Peter Pan*.

"I wore goofy hats to school and did musical theater," he says. "Most people thought I was a dork. But if you have a sense of humor about it, no one can bring you down."

Efron found magic in how a group of people could bring an artistic vision to life onstage. He also found a successful path in life by joining in musical productions, and he gained an appreciation for what it takes to mount a show from start to finish. As a singer and dancer, he was engaged through the three major stage steps—preproduction, rehearsal, and show time. Each stage along the way requires full commitment from crew and cast, including the dancers and choreographers.

Preproduction: Setting the Stage

As people in the audience get swept up in the spectacle of a musical, they may not think about all the long hours that have been invested to bring the show to life. Typically, the entire process begins weeks or months before the first performance. The first step for any theater company is deciding what musical to mount. In many cases, the theater director, music director, and choreographer at a school or community theater put their heads together to decide what show they would like to do. They might make their decision based on how many performers would be involved. Some musicals have big casts of fourteen or more, such as *South Pacific*, *Hairspray*, and *Carousel*. Others can be staged with medium-sized casts of nine to thirteen players, such as *Hair*, *Dirty Rotten Scoundrels*, and *Rent*. There are even some that can have eight or fewer roles, such as *The 25th Annual Putnam County*

To accommodate a large cast size, show producers might select a musical such as *Hairspray*.

Spelling Bee, Little Shop of Horrors, and *Godspell.*
Some shows put the spotlight more on dance and
choreography, including *Fame, Cats, West Side Story,
Thoroughly Modern Millie,* and *The Drowsy Chaperone.*

A theater company must obtain the rights to
perform a show from a publishing or licensing house
such as Dramatists Play Service, Music Theatre
International, or Samuel French. These permissions
and materials can be pricey. One high school in Seattle
had to pay $9,000 to stage *The Sound of Music.* Most
new Broadway musicals are not available for amateurs
because producers believe that other productions
might siphon off ticket sales. Sometimes rights might
not be available if a show is touring or if a motion
picture of the musical is in the works.

No matter what budget they have, the show's
producers are obligated to pay for the rights to the
work to present a public performance.

Once the production team has the score and script
in hand, it wants to become thoroughly familiar with
the material. The choreographer, for example, needs
to fully understand the plot, characters, and character
motivations. Characters may move their bodies
according to their personalities. The Good Witch will
have completely different body language from the Bad
Witch. Choreographers consider how the musical
style of each song should affect the characters'
movements. Should the motions be graceful, such as
in a waltz, or more energetic and almost gymnastic?

West Side Story requires great leaps and turns
in the air. When the two gangs battle, the dancing
is choreographed to convey a fight. During which
scenes should dance be the focus, and how will that

West Side Story puts dancers to a physical test in numbers such as "Cool."

balance against scenes where singing is the center of attention? Some segments will require moving and singing at the same time, so a choreographer has to plan movements that will complement the singers and not leave them too breathless to belt out a tune. A choreographer never wants to inhibit an actor's ability to sing. He or she also plans how dance can be used to transition from scene to scene.

If the musical is a period piece, featuring minuets from the eighteenth century or the twist from the early 1960s, the choreographer may have to do some research. Costuming for a particular era may influence the movement as well.

Nichelle Suzanne, the editor of the website Dance Advantage, says that a director might have no idea what it takes to teach/build/learn choreography. A director usually figures out the blocking during rehearsal, telling actors where they should move for the proper dramatic effect, ensuring **sight lines** for the audience, and working with the lighting design of the scene. The choreographer brings in dance that will mesh with the director's overall vision of blocking. To this end, he or she must discuss each scene and the dancing involved in detail. Ultimately, however, the director leads the entire show, and a choreographer serves to fulfill the director's vision.

A choreographer may refer to previously staged productions of a musical and use those dances, or he or she may develop an original series of motions. A script will have stage directions, and directors must stick with these directions to comply with copyright laws. Watching a movie version of a musical can help. Still, much of the script and how the action and dance unfolds may be left to interpretation.

Suzanne recommends that choreographers watch another version of the musical and then leave it. "The overall impression of the professional version will likely stay with you, helping you to create something that is reminiscent of the original yet uniquely your

Choreographers may draw inspiration from previous productions.

own," she writes. Michael Kerr, the dance instructor at New Voices in Brooklyn, brought his own twist to *Annie*, insisting that it open with a hip-hop techno version of the song "It's a Hard Knock Life." For a production of *Guys and Dolls*, he added a disco-style Cuban piece of choreography.

While a choreographer will want to determine most of the dance before getting together with the performers, some good ideas might come out of **improvisation** with the performers. Leaving some time and room to explore options with the dancers can lead to some good ideas. Ask the actors for their opinions.

Choreographers might think in terms of developing recurring motifs and patterns. While some push to have new motions throughout, repetition and patterns can be effective and rewarding for the audience. For a community or high school program, simplicity may be essential, but still there is room for variety. Keeping the performers facing forward the entire time, for example, can be boring.

As they visualize the musical, choreographers usually take notes on how the musical numbers might unfold and sketch out action. The choreographer consults with the other directors to understand where the performers need to be at the beginning of each scene and where they need to wind up by the end of each scene. The choreographer also may have grand visions for movement, but he or she has to take into consideration the talent level of the dancers. If it's a high school or community theater production, the dance abilities of the cast may be limited.

Choreography can be affected by set design as well. Collaborating with the set designer, a choreographer can come up with motions that blend with the physical items onstage. Depending on how ambitious the production is, dancers may be going up or down stairs—as in the massive group dancing in the musical *42nd Street*. Or they might need to climb scaffolding or perform in a circus-like arena. A *New Yorker* review of *Newsies* shows how challenging dancing can be: "The fifteen or so actors who play the newsies are acrobatic and risk-taking, excelling in huge split leaps and lofty, arcing barrel turns, and clambering artfully around the towering scaffold-like set, a kind of fire-escape hybrid." Understanding the physical space and how it changes throughout the show influences all the dancing.

Dances may depend on costumes as well. *The Lion King* is a great example as the dancers portray animals of the African savanna in costumes that

Newsies requires dancers to race up and down a three-story set, and execute jumps and spins.

JOSH RHODES REALIZES HIS BROADWAY DREAM

When Josh Rhodes was growing up in Decatur, Illinois, he wrote one word in yellow paint on his bedroom wall: "Broadway." As a child, he dreamed of being a dancer in musicals, and he was determined to make that dream become a reality. At age ten, he performed in his first community theater production and had a supportive dance teacher who encouraged him to pursue dance. He did many high school productions and earned a full degree in musical theater from the University of Michigan. Soon after graduation, he moved to New York City and landed his first big gig in a national tour of *Oklahoma.*

"I toured the country for nine months on a bus and I loved it," Rhodes said in an interview for this book. "It was the hardest thing that I've ever done. You woke up early at 5, got on the road, and got to a hotel at 3:30. You would shower, go to a theater, sound check, then do a show. After the performance, you would go to sleep, get up the next day, and do it all over again." Rhodes encourages any young dancer to try an experience like this because it's such good training.

His Broadway debut came when he landed a role in *Fosse,* a musical revue showcasing the choreography of Bob Fosse. "We danced all day long, every single day, as hard as we could," said Rhodes. "At the end of that experience, I felt like I had become a Broadway dancer." He went on to perform in many other productions including *Chicago*, *Sweet Smell of Success* with John Lithgow, *Man of La Mancha* with Brian Stokes Mitchell, and *The Boy from Oz* with Hugh Jackman.

Because Rhodes worked as the dance captain or swing (a member of the company who is an **understudy** for several roles) in several productions, the director and choreographer would turn to him for ideas to assist with the choreography. As he started to do more of it, he thought he might make choreography his profession. When an associate called him to work as the assistant choreographer on a new musical called *The Drowsy Chaperone*, Rhodes jumped at the chance. The show was a hit, and it changed his career. Today, Rhodes is a highly sought-after choreographer who has helped mount productions on Broadway and in the West End of London.

Rhodes feels he is lucky because he is doing what he loves every day. "I love the problem-solving and I love telling stories," he said. "There's never a dull moment."

Since Rhodes has moved from his childhood home, his mother has tried to paint over the word "Broadway" that he had written on his bedroom wall. The word, however, keeps bleeding through the new paint. Just like Rhodes's dream to be a dancer and choreographer, the word does not fade away.

incorporate elements of puppetry. In a musical like *Peter Pan*, the choreographer has to grapple with how to get Peter and the Darling children airborne. Some productions use harnesses and wires. Others simulate flight through other props, lighting, and effects. But in any case, the choreographer has to work closely with the stage manager, stagehands, set designers, and prop handlers to make effects come off seamlessly and blend with any motions.

Another key player who can enhance dances on the stage is the lighting designer. Lights can set a mood or feeling, whether it be harsh, warm, cold, hot, sharp, or fuzzy. Lights can spotlight a specific entertainer or illuminate an entire crowd. Lights can bring color, texture, and shadow. Sidelight helps reveal a dancer s form. Backlight can provide depth. Lights can silhouette figures as well. As the production progresses, the choreographer will want to carefully coordinate the lighting **cues** with the lighting designer. The designer and lighting technicians will follow a specially marked-up script, making sure that illumination is coming on and off, fading and rising, at all the proper moments. Even on a small production, lighting can really add drama to a production in an affordable way.

Auditioning and Casting

The performers make or break a production. Usually, they are chosen through an audition process. In many instances, the producer, director, music director, and choreographer are the deciders. This team begins by reviewing headshots and résumés. Certain roles are simply right for certain looks.

THE TOP HIGH SCHOOL MUSICALS OF 2015–2016

According to a survey from *Dramatics* magazine updated in November 2016, here are the top high school musicals from the 2015–2016 school year.

1. *The Addams Family*
2. *Mary Poppins*
3. *Seussical*
4. *The 25th Annual Putnam County Spelling Bee*
4. (tie) *Cinderella*
6. *Legally Blonde the Musical*
6. (tie) *Grease*
8. *Shrek*
8 (tie) *The Little Mermaid*
10. *Into the Woods*
10. (tie) *Little Shop of Horrors*

For the dancing performers, résumés summarize all the dance training they've had, including at schools, colleges, summer camps, and conservatories, and in after-school programs. Performers present a full account of all related experience—all the musicals in which they've participated, and other related performances, such as plays, music videos, recitals, commercials, skits, revues, and other shows or presentations. Any choreography or teaching experience should be highlighted as well. Include competitions entered and awards won. Think of any skills that might contribute to a role—improvisation, acrobatic and tumbling classes, sports that

Fencing, yoga, martial arts, or other sports improve a dancer's movement.

demonstrate a range of motion (fencing, martial arts, cheerleading, figure skating, yoga, etc.), and singing experiences (in a band, chorus, etc.). A singer can indicate his or her vocal range and type of voice.

The casting team may want to see a recorded sample of a performer in action. YouTube makes it easier than ever to post video clips online. Some dancers and singers will create their own website that displays best performance moments along with résumé details. A person dedicated to dance will want to show range. It's common to demonstrate ability in:

- **Ballet.** A long-established classical dance form defined by precision and highly formalized gestures and leg movements that are fluid and graceful. The art takes years of training to perfect. Techniques include **alignment** (keeping head, shoulders, and hips vertically aligned), **turnout** (a position with legs rotated outward), and **pointe work** (supporting the entire body weight on the tips of fully extended feet while wearing pointe shoes). Men and women with ballet training typically have some background in partnering. Many scenes in musicals involve dancing in a duet.

- **Jazz dance.** A type of movement that showcases individual style and originality. It is distinguished by interpretation, energy, fun, and fancy footwork.

- **Modern dance.** A free, expressive dance style for conveying abstract ideas. It encourages artistic individualism, the inner self, and complex emotions. Movements do not always match rhythms. Some use this style of dance for social commentary or to tell stories.

- **Tap dance.** Often used in musicals, this form is characterized by creating percussive sounds with special tap shoes that rhythmically strike the floor.

Jazz dance, in particular, has evolved to suit the needs of the Broadway musical. George Balanchine, Jerome Robbins, and Bob Fosse are among the top choreographers who have brought their signature technical skills, movements, and vocabulary to the musical using jazz dance. Those seriously looking to perform in musical theater can benefit from dance classes because they will learn the techniques expected in the professional dance world and learn the terms that dancers use. Most productions will want those auditioning to demonstrate competent dancing from the outset and understand the language of dance.

Once the director and choreographer have narrowed down their top selections for the cast, they will call performers in to do a live audition. Performers staging a musical must be able to stand the pressure of performing live, and an audition puts that to the test. For the candidate, it's emotional, nerve-wracking, exciting, challenging, and often overwhelming. A singer/dancer has to step before a small panel of judges and, within a few minutes, give a convincing sample of his or her talents. The choreographer will often evaluate dancers in an audition that is strictly about the dance. A group of dancers may learn a short combination on the spot and audition together.

Those auditioning have a chance to show off their people skills and make a personal connection with the core team. For the serious dancer/singer, auditions are part of the work landscape. If you pursue this as a career, build a tough skin and brace yourself for a lot of rejection. In show biz, more rejections usually lead to more successes and more roles in the long run. Try to learn from failures, but don't take rejection too hard—there are plenty more auditions ahead.

Appearance Is Important

To succeed at an audition, preparation is the main ingredient. Appearance will make the first impression, so when auditioning, dress appropriately. For dancers, this can often mean wearing body-hugging attire that shows off one's physique. The audition may specify exactly what to wear, but **leotards** and tights are a standard wardrobe. Jazz shorts are a possibility. Leave the flip-flops at home. Dance shoes are a must. The production may require ballet slippers, jazz shoes, tap shoes, or even heels. A production of *Hair*, for example, might have some barefoot dancing. The

Each show will have its own style of dance, such as jazz.

message is to be ready for anything. A choreographer may ask to see you do a brief solo that highlights your strengths but will also support the particular production. For example, the smash Broadway musical *Hamilton* features hip-hop, and a traveling production of this show would want potential cast members to demonstrate their hip-hop chops while wearing boots.

In general, those casting want to see faces—long hair needs to be pulled back from the face, and when dancing, hair can't be flying into the eyes and mouth. For women, some makeup can be helpful, but don't overdo it. Most jewelry—earrings, rings, necklaces—should be removed. Perfumes and colognes are a negative, but deodorant is a positive. Keep everything neutral when it comes to appearance.

You will not only have to be literally fast on your feet, but also mentally fast on your feet. If a choreographer throws a request at you, you have to be attentive, focused, and able to deliver. This will show that you're able to follow direction, and that can make a difference in whether you get cast or not. But if you don't understand a request, don't hesitate to ask a question. Be sure to project confidence. People want to see that you feel comfortable in your own skin. If you believe in yourself, so will others. Also, show your personality—it's what sets you apart from others.

Dancing is a very collaborative art, so you might have to audition with a partner or while interacting in a group.

In addition to showing off dance prowess, if you are auditioning for a musical you will probably have to demonstrate singing ability as well. A pianist may be in the room to accompany those trying out. During your vocal audition, be polite and friendly to the

When it comes to auditioning, dress appropriately for the role and put your best foot forward.

accompanist—sometimes he or she has a voice in the decision process. Often an audition just gives time to sing sixteen to thirty-two bars because so many are trying out.

To reduce the stress, get a good night's rest and eat a healthy breakfast. Be sure to arrive early, giving yourself time to stretch and warm up. You want muscles primed and flexibility at its peak. If you've been taking any sort of dance classes, you probably have some warm-up exercises to follow, but you can find many online if you need some. Arriving early may also give you an advantage—you want to sign in and make sure you have a spot. Plus, arriving early has the potential to cut down on the time worrying and waiting.

Some meditative practice can ease the tension—breathe and give yourself a pep talk: "I can do this." Remember to stay positive and confident throughout—casting directors can catch the slightest whiff of flop sweat. Don't forget to thank everyone in the room when finished.

Even if an actor is lucky to get a call from the casting team, the auditioning process might not be over. The call may be for a **callback** so those casting can see some additional performance. A callback means you're progressing toward getting the position, but you haven't quite landed the gig yet.

Down to Business: Rehearsals

Those fortunate to be chosen to star in the cast then enter the next step for mounting a theatrical production. This is the rehearsal stage, and it is the most demanding. Typically, a musical follows a rehearsal schedule of six to eight weeks, although some stage productions have an intensive four-week rehearsal period while others may require more than two months to get everything right. Everyone involved in the show will be given the schedule detailing the days and hours they are expected to be available. A school or community production demands that students put in hours after class and on the weekends. To maintain sanity among the cast, directors and choreographers make sure not to overload their performers and give them days off as well. Some of the scheduled days have to have a flexible agenda, especially as the performance dates get closer. This gives the director a chance to focus on the parts that need the most work.

To stage a professional show with few mistakes, the rehearsal process is critical and requires absolute commitment—not just from the dancers and choreographer, but from all who are involved. All participants will be given a schedule, and in many productions, even those at high schools and community theaters, performers are asked to sign letters of commitment. Directors use these to underscore how serious the effort is. By signing, the actor or dancer agrees to show up on time for all rehearsals, performances, and requested activities. The fact is, if someone drops out, an entire production could be in jeopardy.

If a lead performer suddenly gets sick or quits, a musical can especially be in trouble. That's why directors usually cast understudies who know all the songs and dance moves of the stars. In 1972, the actor

Richard Gere was the understudy for several roles in a New York version of *Grease*. He had all the moves and songs memorized perfectly, so when he stepped into the lead role of Danny Zuko one night, he wowed the crowd. For Gere, it was a lucky break, and he went on to star in the show in London. In a similar way, Shirley MacLaine got her big break when she stepped into the starring role singing and dancing her way through *The Pajama Game*.

Before the performers arrive on day one, dancers who may be singing as well should be familiar with the script and score. If there has been enough time, performers have begun to memorize their lines and lyrics.

As the choreographer begins rehearsals, he or she has to be in perfect sync with the director and the music director. Dance numbers can't be too short or too long—they have to be in perfect unison with the music.

Coming Together

In many productions, the entire cast and crew will come together for an initial meeting to create a sense of team unity. When all participants have a chance to meet and introduce themselves, it builds team spirit. Often, the director will guide the cast through an entire read-through on this first day.

In the early stages, rehearsals often break up into different groups and segments. The musicians will be practicing separately from the performers. The tech crew will be meeting to discuss and review their roles. Performers may have rehearsals for the songs and the acting that are separate from the dance numbers. Some dance rehearsals may involve the full ensemble, while others may focus on solos, duets, or smaller group numbers.

In a first dance rehearsal, the choreographer will establish his or her rules and expectations, which usually means being on time and coming prepared. One common rule is cell phones must be turned off during practice—they can be disruptive and a distraction. The choreographer may specify what types of clothes and shoes to wear to rehearsals and suggest bringing kneepads, headbands, and other items that will ease the rehearsing. He or she will often take down all contact information, emergency contacts, and any health concerns (allergies, epilepsy, diabetes, etc.). Choreographers make it clear that their vision and instructions are to be followed in terms of dance steps, but they are open to suggestions.

The performers need to come equipped to survive the long hours. Intensive, repetitive motions can build a thirst, so dancers should carry their own water bottle. While hydration is vital, so is fuel. In fact, a choreographer might ask the dancers to bring food. Rehearsals can run long and be most productive when there are no extended breaks. Think about what types of food will not weigh the body down but provide energy—carrots, apples, peanut butter, energy bars, nuts, etc. Naturally, all the exertion leads to perspiration—dancers should bring a hand towel and make sure to wear deodorant.

Before a review of the actual dance steps begins, the performers need to warm up their bodies. They usually limber up by stretching and running through

> A dancer's body is his or her instrument. It must be warmed up to perform well.

some exercises. Without warming up, a dancer can pull a muscle or be unable to execute certain moves. The choreographer may set up a routine for this and possibly lead it.

Getting Loose

The Rockettes, the famous New York City dance troupe, warm up with shoulder, rib, pelvis, wrist, and ankle rolls; brisk walking, jumping jacks, or small jumps in place; light jogging, marching, prancing, and skipping (around the room or in place); lunges across the floor or a large Charleston step; and push-ups. They also spend five to ten minutes doing **lengthening**, full-body motions: reaching and

MAKING DANCE A CAREER

Brenna Monroe-Cook grew up in Oak Park, Illinois, with dreams of becoming a dancer. Her dedication to pursuing that dream made her childhood wishes into a reality. Her hometown may have influenced Monroe-Cook. Doris Humphrey, the renowned dancer and choreographer, and a contemporary of choreographers Martha Graham and Katherine Dunham, was born in Oak Park, and the locals hold her in high regard. Although Monroe-Cook started her studies with ballet, she also learned jazz, modern, **flamenco**, and other styles.

"I learned that all styles were of equal importance, and that has influenced me to this day," she says. Monroe-Cook attended dance camps, including one at the prestigious Joffrey Ballet. Wanting to be a serious dancer, she auditioned for the Juilliard School of Dance, Drama, and Music in her junior year of high school. She didn't get in but was given notes and encouraged to try again the following year. Determined to gain admission, Monroe-Cook tried out again and got in.

bending up, over, forward, and sideways (try one-leg variations to challenge **core stability** and balance); large arm swings or circles with torso twisting; dynamic (moving) series of bridges or other yoga poses; body (torso) swings; and leg swings standing or leg-drop swings lying on your back on the floor.

For some shows, it is productive to have two work rooms—one where a choreographer might

After graduating, she waitressed and met the director of the Limón Dance Company. Her audition went well, and she joined the company.

When preparing for a show, she typically gets to the rehearsal space for morning class from 9:00 to 10:30 to train and warm up her body. The rest of the day, until 5:00 p.m., is usually dedicated to rehearsing and perfecting the dances. Her troupe performs in New York City but also takes many trips to present its work throughout the United States and around the world.

After working just with the company for five years, she wanted some relief from the city life of New York. She found work teaching and performing in Seattle. Today, Monroe-Cook has found an ideal balance in her life, and it all revolves around her passion for dance. She continues to perform with the Limón Dance Company part of the year, and she returns to work in Seattle the rest of the year.

work with and teach specific performers, and then another where other cast members can go off and work independently. As the rehearsals progress, the choreographer has to take notes and make sure that the performers are evolving and that goals are being met. The choreographer notes what parts need more of his or her attention and which ones can be rehearsed independently.

By a few rehearsals in, the choreographer may begin to incorporate spoken lines of **dialogue** and singing with the dance moves. The music director or lead director might participate in these rehearsals as well so the songs, spoken lines, and **characterization** can be smoothly incorporated with the motions. A pianist may be in rehearsals as well—in high school productions this might be the music director—although some productions will rely on prerecorded music. The dance takes on more meaning as performers gain a better sense of mood and character motivation. To steadily build each number to performance-level energy, the choreographer might be shouting words of encouragement—like a coach—pushing the actors to give it their all. Positive reinforcement can go a long way toward getting people to give their best. By the same token, toughness pays off as well. If the choreographer is not seeing the expected results, he or she needs to have the cast do it again and again until some progress is achieved.

Often by the three-week mark, performers are working **off book.** This means they are no longer clutching scripts; they have their lines memorized. It's to be expected that they might not have everything down pat, so someone offstage will be in charge of feeding lines to the actors if they have a memory lapse.

After going through scenes, it's standard practice for the choreographer and director to give notes to improve dance steps and line delivery. Sometimes, a cast member must be pulled aside privately so he or she can be given personalized guidance. Directing notes might concern a delivery that is too low in

Before the dress rehearsal, entertainers put in hours and hours of practice to perfect a show.

volume, lacking in emotion, rushed, or mumbled, or that gives an appearance of not listening to another actor. Choreographers will often ask for cast input as well to get their take on where they might be struggling or discover ideas that can heighten the performance. The performers should also keep their own written notes to remind them of parts they need to improve.

From Tech to Dress Rehearsal

As the performance dates draw closer, time needs to be allotted for the performers to try their makeup and costumes. More elaborate productions will have a hairdresser and a makeup artist who will develop the look of all the characters, and the dancer will have to spend time with them so these crew members can work their magic. In a similar way, costume designers will take body measurements of performers to create the outfits and then work closely with the actor when the costumes are ready, making any adjustments so the performers will not have any trouble moving about onstage.

For many high school and community theater productions, the actors and dancers have to handle their own costumes, piecing together what they can from their closets or local thrift shops. They might handle their own makeup as well. In musicals especially, costumers revisit with the performers to make sure garments are holding up after repeated vigorous motions. Buttons can't pop; fabrics can't tear; zippers cannot come undone. They also have to accommodate portable microphones and transmitters that might be attached to performers' bodies.

A week or so before the first performance date, the director may schedule **tech rehearsals.** A tech rehearsal brings together all the players and technical crew to run through the entire show. Dancers have time to get accustomed to the stage during these rehearsals, although they do not have to be in full dress. They see their marks where they should stop and deliver lines, sing, or deliver a certain dance routine. The lighting technicians will run through their cues with the live performers. They adjust the lights to the proper positions and assure the timing is correct. All wiring has to be connected properly and must not interfere with any of the action on the stage. A lot of stopping, restarting, and repeating may be needed as the tech crew makes adjustments.

Sound technicians will work closely with singers/dancers, fitting them with microphones and testing the audio equipment, checking that voices are heard and transmissions are problem-free. In today's musical theater world, performers usually wear mic packs for cordless transmission of sound. A mic pack has a transmitter that is basically the size of a deck of cards and runs on batteries. Techs must make sure that the batteries are fresh and will not die, or there will be no sound in the audience. A microphone is attached somewhere near the singer's mouth. A thin wire runs from it to the transmitter pack hidden somewhere in the actor's costume. The transmitter sends an audio signal to a central receiver, which then sends the sound to speakers in the theater. It's essential for tech to review that all this works right. And as singers move about, especially in dance numbers, they need to know that their mic packs are securely attached to their bodies. Solving technical issues can take time, so dancers/performers must have patience.

Note that performers might not have to give a full-on performance as the technicians adjust their equipment. They may want to conserve energy and voices. Sound techs may run any prerecorded music and sound effects as well, and the players have a chance to see how these will tie in with the live show.

Set designers may be on hand for tech rehearsals. Players have to run through their motions with all props and set pieces in place as well. Placement of furniture, doorways, backgrounds, curtains, etc., can influence how motions will unfold onstage. Sometimes rehearsals take place onstage before all stage sets are constructed, so a stage manager may mark off in tape where set items will be placed. The actors work around these marks until the real items are ready.

Once tech problems are worked out, a production will then move on to a full-on dress rehearsal that presents the entire show as it should be from top to bottom, with all crew present and performers in costume. Musicals need at least one tech rehearsal but often two or more. The dress rehearsal puts all the balls in motion—sets are moving; curtains are rising and dropping; lights are dimming, brightening, flashing; sound effects are triggered; the music flows, and musicians are all playing their parts correctly; and all performers carry the story from start to finish without pause. It's a last chance to correct any issues with any element.

Get a Good Look

The choreographer should sit in the audience during these rehearsals and confirm that everything looks and sounds correct from the house. It's smart to view the show from different seats in the audience to make sure sight lines are clear. Also, these views can reveal that the dancers need adjustment when it comes to spacing. They may look too crowded or too far apart.

It might seem unnecessary, but all shows should take time to rehearse the bows and **curtain call** as well. This final thank-you to the crowd has to look just as professional as the rest of the show.

Some companies decide to do a practice performance in front of an audience—similar to having a preview on Broadway. While the audience doesn't have to be as big as for a real show, a crowd of any size can provide reactions that can reveal what's working and what's not.

For many directors, it's customary to have an entire day and night off between the final dress rehearsal and the first performance. Those who follow this custom say that singers come in with rested voices, dancers have more energy, and the whole crew is more on the ball.

The Curtain Rises

After weeks and weeks of hard work, the big moment finally arrives. For the dancers and performers who started long ago by passing the audition process, this is the payoff for all their hard work. A choreographer will want to be backstage before the show to give the dancers a final pep talk for confidence, just like a coach. The nervous energy among performers can be intense, but it means **adrenaline** is flowing and it can fuel a great performance. Having some butterflies in your stomach is only natural, and performers often do a lot of deep breathing beforehand to avoid getting overwhelmed with stage fright.

All sound technicians, costume helpers, makeup artists, prop handlers, and lighting and stage crew members must arrive early for final checks. Someone in the crew should be in charge of videotaping the performance. Performers may want to review the tape later to see how things went and make any tweaks in

An applauding audience provides the payoff for all the hard work that goes into a successful musical.

their acting or dancing. Actors need to arrive with plenty of time to get into makeup and costumes. Just as before rehearsals, dancers and singers have to go through warm-up exercises. Some will drift off into the corners backstage to review lines.

Before the curtain rises, the choreographer will want to check that the dancers are all set and in place, ready to go. The stage manager will review that all crew members are in position. Often, a wardrobe person will be in the wings to help cast members get in and out of garments but also to make any quick repairs. Makeup people may be in position during the show for the same reasons—for changes in looks and touch-ups. Everyone backstage has to remember to keep quiet—no chatting, no phones, no noise.

Musicals are notorious for costume changes, so performers have to be ready for their quick transformations. They need to keep careful track of exactly where all their costumes are so that they can do some fast undressing and dressing. If a dancer takes a stumble or forgets a part, he or she must remember the old entertainment saying: "The show must go on." Audiences are forgiving—pick yourself up, find your place, and get back in the flow.

When the show ends, one of the biggest rewards comes as the audience wildly applauds. After the curtain goes down and bows are taken, cast and crew might convene backstage for some notes from the director or choreographer. Also, in school and community groups, cast and crew may have roles in cleanup and readying everything for the next day's performance. When the entire run ends, the company will gather together for a cast party to celebrate their success.

For serious dancers, the action doesn't stop with the end of a show. They continue with attending classes, workshops, concerts, and other shows. They review their performance, thinking about what they enjoyed most, what they would like to work on, and how they might challenge themselves next time.

Ethel Merman took a tumble during *Call Me Madam* but kept right on singing.

CHAPTER FOUR

Making It Past the Missteps

Musical theater has so many moving parts that it seems almost inevitable that mistakes will happen. Occasionally, the pitfalls are literally that. There have been a number of real incidents when dancers have taken a misstep and actually fallen into the orchestra pit.

Singer and dancer Manoel Felciano was one of those unfortunate few. He had a regular role in *Jesus Christ Superstar* as one of the disciples, and he understudied as Judas. When the regular Judas took ill one night, Felciano stepped in—perhaps not entirely as prepared as he should have been. Near the end of his first song, the powerful "Heaven on Their Minds," Felciano rushed with great fervor to the front of the stage and suddenly disappeared. Some in the audience gasped as they heard a body fall. As the orchestra hesitantly finished the song, the crowd looked on in concern and expectation. As the next number began, however, the conductor helped boost Felciano back on the stage. The relieved audience went crazy with applause.

While mistakes among dancers may not always be that dramatic, it does highlight the fact that audiences are forgiving. So while performers often worry about possible mistakes, the crowd is generally rooting for the performer and wants him or her to succeed. They are supportive. Performers always have to remember to keep going if the unexpected happens.

Costume Catastrophes

Because dancers are involved in such vigorous motions, costumes have the potential to break down, rip, get stuck, or fall apart. On YouTube, a clip from a high school production of *Singin' in the Rain* at Dr. Phillips High School in Orlando shows the lead struggling to keep his fly up, but to his credit he keeps on dancing despite unexpected laughter from the audience. An article in the *Ballet Bag* recounts how during a production of *Sleeping Beauty* in Canada some years ago, the head of wardrobe saw the female Bluebird running offstage clutching at her costume in despair. "The fabric of her tutu had ripped and she had literally fallen out of the bottom of her tutu! After some quick work with a safety pin, the Bluebird was back on stage in time for her next entrance."

While singing onstage at Radio City Music Hall, Broadway star Idina Menzel had a very revealing moment with her low-cut silver gown. She took the right approach about her overexposure—joking about it, fixing the situation, and continuing on.

During the San Francisco previews for *Legally Blonde the Musical*, Laura Bell Bundy's shoe went flying into the audience following a particularly enthusiastic high kick. Without missing a beat, she continued the song and choreography while removing

Colorful costumes enhance any musical, but vigorous motions or missteps can cause damage.

her other shoe and hurling that one into the audience, too. She finished the song barefoot. It probably helped that she was only about forty-five seconds away from the curtain falling for the end of act 1, but still the audience was impressed with her fast thinking and smooth save.

PICK YOURSELF UP AND GET BACK IN THE RACE

Brenna Monroe-Cook knows the horror of things going wrong onstage. One of her most memorable onstage mishaps happened when performing a German expressionist dance piece in Berlin. Titled *Extreme Beauty*, the dance was a meditation on the bizarre things that women do in the name of beauty. Monroe-Cook was in an ensemble of female dancers who were all wearing high-heeled shoes on their heads like they were hats, and long, big hoop skirts. Although she was fitted for the skirt and had practiced with it, the outfits were awkward to move in. She did tiny shuffling steps in front of a crowd in a two-thousand-seat theater.

"My hoop skirt was just a little too long though," she says. "I tripped on it and recovered and kept shuffling along and tripped on it again and kept shuffling along and tripped on it a third time and fell down on my face. I tried to stand up in a normal way but I couldn't—the hoop skirt was in the way. Every

Sometimes makeup can distract from a performance as well. Dancer and singer Rodney Hicks recalls his initial audition for *Rent* in December of 1995. He was twenty-one but looked seventeen. To look older, he decided to use mascara and draw on a goatee. He couldn't grow facial hair at the time. After executing a back flip as part of a hip-hop dance, the goatee sweated off. When he took off his red cardigan time I would try to get up, I'd be stepping on the skirt. I finally had to roll on my back and get my legs in the air and swing my legs so I could boost myself up. The woman next to me said she thought she should fall down too to make it look like it was meant to be part of the choreography."

Monroe-Cook says it was embarrassing, but she knew the show had to go on, so she figured out a way to get back up and keep going. She says mistakes are part of the landscape with live performance. During another show, she was dancing on a set meant to look like a big mausoleum. All the stone walls were made of Styrofoam. When one of the other dancers did a big leaping jump through what was supposed to be a heavy door, she accidentally knocked the Styrofoam door off of its hinges. It flew off much too easily. She just had to keep dancing. The audience laughed. "How do you move on once the mistake happens?" says Monroe-Cook. "You have to move on and laugh it off."

sweater, the fake beard wiped off even more. Hicks is sure casting must have noticed, but they still liked his performance and he landed the role.

A classic episode of the public radio show *This American Life* titled "Fiasco" recounts one of the biggest theater disasters ever during a production of *Peter Pan*. Everything that could go horribly wrong did go horribly wrong. Jack Hitt tells the story of a

In shows such as *Peter Pan*, the wiring must be carefully checked to avoid accidents.

staging he saw in 1973 at an unnamed local college. When the kids in the musical were sprinkled with magic dust that should make them fly, they jerked up in the air a bit and then hung like puppets. Hitt says that everyone was afraid for the dangling actors and gripping their chairs nervously. One kid singer crashed into a wardrobe as his wire swung out of control. When Captain Hook took the stage, things seemed to calm down. Although the actor was in total command, he gestured too vigorously and sent his hook flying off his hand and into the audience, socking an old lady in the gut. Thinking fast, the actor playing Hook told the crowd, "You know, they just don't make those hooks like they used to." The **ad lib** saved the moment.

Later in the show, Peter Pan and the kids flew into Neverland, landing hard on the stage and then being dragged in such a way that wiped out some of the set. When one actor then fell from a balcony and injured himself, someone pulled an alarm, and shortly thereafter fifteen local firemen wearing boots and hats and dragging hoses came busting into the theater. It was one of the most nerve-wracking nights of theater ever.

Battling Against Bodily Harm

Daniel Curry, twenty-three, was one of nine dancers in *Spider-Man: Turn Off the Dark*. One night, he stepped into the wrong position at the back of the Foxwoods Theatre stage and became snared in a hydraulic stage lift, severely injuring his foot. Leading actor Christopher Tierney suffered life-threatening injuries in the same musical when he fell more than 30 feet (9.1 meters) from a platform into the orchestra pit in December 2010.

For dancers, however, difficulties can go beyond the slip-ups that might occur during a performance. When working as a dancer in musicals, the body can take a regular beating. The leaps, rolls, slides, and other maneuvers can take a toll physically. Some dancers have jumped, landed, and heard an unpleasant pop. Dance work is rigorous, and it's not unusual for a dancer to sprain an ankle, bruise a muscle, or break a bone. According to the Bureau of Labor Statistics, dancing has one of the highest nonfatal job-related

Dancing is a bruising profession. *Lord of the Dance* creator Michael Flatley had to retire after his body suffered years of wear and tear.

injury rates of any profession. In 2015, Michael Flatley, who created the hit shows *Lord of the Dance* and *Riverdance*, retired at age fifty-seven because of the grueling impact that dancing had taken on his body. He had suffered broken bones and spine damage over the years. Many dancers retire in their thirties.

Dancers' bodies simply take a pounding, and a wrong move can end a career prematurely or slow it down. Rickey Tripp was an ensemble member in Broadway's *In the Heights*. He had to leave the production for ten months, however, because repeated stress gave him **tendinitis** in the hip. Megan Richardson, a licensed physical therapist at the Harkness Center for Dance Injuries at New York University, said in an article in *Backstage* that 65 percent of dance injuries are from overuse and repetitive stress. Some show schedules are super demanding, and that leads to muscle fatigue. Along with grueling performance schedules, stage conditions and costume weight can play a role. A young dancer who is heavily involved in school or community musicals has to pay close attention to his or her body. Proper exercise, diet, and sleep can help bodies stay strong and flexible.

Another difficulty for dancers is simply landing the work. Getting regular jobs dancing in theater, even on a local level, requires constant auditioning and constant rejection. The field is highly competitive, and there can be big gaps between shows. Those who seriously pursue the field might have to work other jobs that give them the flexibility to audition and perform when opportunity knocks. That's why many dancers take on work as a waiter or bartender.

Often the best jobs are through entertainment-related unions such as AEA, SAG-AFTRA, and AGMA, which ensure good wages, access to better working conditions, and pension and health insurance benefits.

Dancer Etiquette

Dancers are expected to conduct themselves with class and be polite toward one another. According to the Academy of Performing Arts in Sault Ste. Marie, Michigan, dancers must always strive to be artistic, intelligent, musical, and graceful, and to present themselves with great self-control. Dancers listen quietly and respectfully to instructors and directors. Still, they may also ask questions, and this type of inquiry can only improve their performance. The most respected dancers do not whine, gossip, or complain; they support and encourage other dancers. They also show regard for dance by wearing the right attire for rehearsals. They arrive to rehearse or perform with a tidy and clean appearance.

There are many expectations of behavior for dance classes and rehearsals. Punctuality is at the top of the list. You must consider everyone else's time, and if you're late, you're not showing respect for that. Plus, arriving late disrupts the flow of a practice or lesson. If you're going to be late or absent, call and give warning. Be prepared for whatever the session for that day involves.

In an interview for this book, Lonny Price, a veteran director whose productions include Andrew Lloyd Webber's *Sunset Boulevard* and a 2017 production of *Carousel* in London, said, "Here's what

Dancers are expected to follow certain etiquette, such as wearing proper clothing and not blocking another's view of the mirror.

I say to everybody on the first day of rehearsal: 'Behind you is a line of one hundred people who wish they could be here, but you're lucky. You're the one who got to be here, and because of that you have a responsibility to do your best, show up on time, and work hard for that person who is waiting tables that didn't get to be here today. It is an honor to work in the theater. You have to be prepared, work hard, be on time, and take this seriously because those of us who have been doing this for a long time do take it seriously. The theater deserves your respect.'"

An article titled "10 Tips for Successful Dance Auditions" from musical-creations.com recommends that dancers never stand at the back of the studio during an audition. Instead, dancers should always stand on the sides. The article also advises that you never dance full out until it is your turn. "It distracts the team and is very disrespectful to the people who are on at that point," the article states.

The website Musical Theatre U features an article titled "Dance Class Etiquette 101" that offers plenty of solid advice on how to act in dance classes and auditions. It says that during class, being aware of personal space is a must, especially when a room is full of dancers in motion. Try not to stand uncomfortably close to someone if there is room to spread out. Some dancers will jockey for space in the front or in the middle, but to assure a preferred spot, arrive early. If there is a mirror for looking at your movements, try not to block anyone else's view. Avoid sudden stops in a routine because they can lead to crashing bodies in the ensemble. If there is confusion about the steps required, politely ask. It's necessary to clear up any uncertainty during a rehearsal before moving on.

Dancers, as with all stage cast and crew, need to follow some general rules.

Remind anyone that you know who is coming to a performance to arrive about a half hour before show time. People need to be seated before houselights go down and curtains come up. Arriving late can cause a distraction.

Before the show, performers should not mingle with audience members. It ruins some of the magic of live theater and takes away from the performance.

Dancers must remain quiet backstage so their voices don't interfere with the show. Just like audience members, dancers need to turn off their cell phones or set them to silent. Do not cause a disruption by taking any flash photography.

Dancers should not linger in the wings to watch the show because they can wind up in the way and be a distraction. If dancers are in the wings, they should be waiting to make an entrance, often hidden behind curtains called legs.

Dancers are advised to keep their dressing areas neat and clean. They need to double-check that all costumes and props are in place and at the ready before show time.

At all times, dancers need to be attentive, give their best, and always be respectful to everyone in the theater.

Dancers should seek opportunities to perform beyond the stage.

CHAPTER FIVE

Taking Steps into the Real World

A lucky, hardworking, talented few build careers as dancers. It's not impossible to do so, but it can be difficult. As the musical director Lonny Price says, "This is a very hard business, it's full of disappointment, there's no job security, and there's no financial security."

Some dancers who want to keep a foot in the business may look beyond the worlds of musical theater and dance companies. Dancers also find work in Las Vegas productions, amusement parks, and on cruise lines. They pick up work in movies, television shows, and music videos.

The experience of dancing in theater, however, can give an individual skills that he or she can take into other "real world" opportunities and use to find gainful employment and a rewarding career path.

Gaining Transferable Skills

Anyone who joins in a school or theater production will learn the value of teamwork, working with other people with different personalities and talents who come together to achieve a common goal.

Musical theater work encourages collaboration and demonstrates that an individual has the ability to get along well with others. Gus Moody, a high school student in New York City, found that dancing and singing in musicals boosted his confidence and his ability to work with others and talk to strangers.

Those who have been immersed in a few musical theater productions build many soft skills that the business world craves. Theater people are problem solvers who don't hesitate to take on sudden troubles and come up with creative solutions. They are often perfectionists who will settle for nothing less than the best. Plus, they learn to stay calm in a crisis.

They often acquire a positive, can-do attitude that inspires coworkers. They have a history of hard work and are usually eager to put in extra time. Also, while theater people are incredibly hardworking, they also like to have fun.

The theater experience makes them strong communicators. Some dancers will have to deliver lines in front of a crowd, which can give them the confidence to speak before groups in other settings. Learning to effectively communicate a message can help with job interviews, business meetings, presentations, and speeches. By merely watching other actors deliver lines, dancers can learn how to create dramatic effects and capture attention by raising and lowering their voices. They can also learn how to command a room by moving their body. These techniques can help in all sorts of careers, from lawyer to politician to corporate executive.

An article in *Dramatics* magazine features interviews with CEOs who spoke about why they like to hire people who have been involved in theater productions. One said, "Theatre students have done extremely well with us and we usually hire them because they're well-disciplined workers who learn quickly and give of themselves to the company." Another added, "We like to hire theatre students but it is a shame that when they apply to us they don't seem to realize their strengths and advantages."

From the Boards to the Boardroom

Katie Ailes, who double-majored in English and dance in college, writes online that studying and perfecting dance instills a sense of discipline that all businesses value and helps an individual reach personal goals and achieve more. Dedicated dancers bring self-control and organization to all aspects of their lives—they focus on their diet, their sleep, their exercise. They schedule their lives carefully to fit in academic classes, dance instruction, and rehearsal time. They are proof that regular commitment leads to improvement and that learning builds skills and produces results. All businesses want people who will diligently work toward goals with the type of focus that dancers have. When bosses hire a dancer, they know they are getting an employee with a strong work ethic. Theater is deadline-oriented as well, and constantly involves quality control.

Dancers develop punctuality because they must get to all classes, practices, rehearsals, and performances on time. If they're not there as

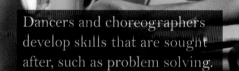

Dancers and choreographers develop skills that are sought after, such as problem solving.

expected, they let others down. Rehearsals cannot happen if dancers are not in their places and ready to go at the appointed hour. Dancers who have been in several productions are determined and not quitters. They have weathered rejection and have forged on. Theater is a field that requires hustle, and hustle is a quality that can improve any operation.

Ailes says that choreographers have additional talents that the corporate world may seek. Choreographers know how to innovate. While there is a respect for the rules, they can take established techniques and methods, and apply them in new ways, coming up with entirely new approaches and visions. They use research to inform new work—a quality that is certainly highly regarded in the world of academia.

Choreographers also have leadership skills. They have the ability to motivate, organize, and direct. They can instruct a group on what actions are needed to achieve a goal. They keep the team on task and focused. They can identify weaknesses in individuals and guide them to be stronger performers. Their words can bring a vitality, energy, inspiration, and purpose to a group. Employers want leaders who can get the absolute best out of workers, and that's what choreographers do.

Choreographers grasp related art forms that support their work—they understand how lighting, costuming, makeup, stage management, props, sets, and sound all tie into the bigger picture of producing a show. The ability to grasp and juggle multiple aspects of an operation is a highly transferable skill.

Choreographers and dancers develop a knack for self-promotion. They learn to sell themselves. They may have a hand in raising money, renting theaters, balancing a budget, and advertising a show. Getting art to a paying audience is how theater survives. All this develops business savvy that even business-school graduates may not have had a chance to hone.

Some dancers and choreographers have such an intimate knowledge of the theater world that they shift to closely related careers—stage management, theater marketing and promotion, grant writing, finance for arts organizations, facilities operations, theater company web design, costume design, hair and makeup, or special events planning, for example. Some may gain experience working with set construction and find work later as a builder, woodworker, electrician, or painter.

You never know where early experience with dance may take you. American billionaire Mark Cuban spent time at Indiana University teaching disco dancing. He charged twenty-five dollars, and it demonstrated his entrepreneurial spirit. Leigh Thomas, director of global accounts for Facebook, credits the discipline she learned as a ballerina for her success in the business world.

Many dancers go on to teach the art itself. They may give private lessons or share their knowledge at a grade school, high school, or college. They might find opportunities with community theaters or school theater productions.

A Route into Acting

Some dance workshops focus on dance movements for actors. Any actor can benefit from knowing how to use his or her body for more dramatic effect. Dance can make actors more graceful. Dancers learn to convey emotions with body position and movement. Some dancers, in fact, become effective actors, including Summer Glau, Mia Wasikowska, Lea Thompson, Penélope Cruz, Neve Campbell, and Alexander Godunov. Channing Tatum made his screen debut as a dancer in Ricky Martin's "She Bangs" video. By studying jazz, ballet, and Latin dance, Zoe Saldana developed a physicality that led her to roles in many sci-fi action movies, including *Guardians of the Galaxy* and *Avatar*. The veteran actor Christopher Walken started as a musical theater dancer and went on to be a huge movie star. He put his dance chops to the test in the memorable 2001

Christopher Walken and John Travolta showed their dancing prowess in the 2007 film version of *Hairspray*.

music video for the Fatboy Slim song "Weapon of Choice." Jennifer Lopez started as a dancer and singer and successfully transitioned to the world of acting.

Sometimes a dancer has to step in and **double** for an actor who might not be able to pull off the steps. Kevin Bacon did the majority of his own dancing in the movie *Footloose*, but he had a dance double and two gymnastics doubles for some scenes.

Dance training can help someone enter the world of stage combat and possibly stunt work.

A lot of action films and live theater require choreographed fight scenes, and dancers are the pros at choreographing motions. There's a structure to a fight that is like a dance, and the moves are done over and over again until they become second nature.

Helping Other Bodies Stay in Motion

Dancers might find specific work training athletes as well. Steve McLendon, a nose tackle who has played for the Pittsburgh Steelers and the New York Jets, began taking ballet in his senior year at Troy University in Alabama in 2009. He has said that it's harder than anything else he has done, but ballet has helped him stay injury-free by strengthening his knees, ankles, and feet. A 2013 article in *Psychology Today* reported that regular aerobic training incorporated with some type of dance at least once a week could help anyone maximize his or her brain function.

Because dancers are so physical, some turn to jobs in personal training, athletic coaching, or group fitness. They may instruct yoga, spin classes, or other exercise regimens. Some other more recent physical programs that might suit dancers include **Feldenkrais Method**, **Gyrotonic movement**, and **Somatic exercise.**

Because dancers are accustomed to being physical with other people, some turn to careers such as massage therapist, physical therapist, and occupational therapist. There is also dance therapy that combines both dance and physical therapy.

Later in life, dancers may transition into careers in fitness instruction, teaching yoga, Pilates, or another physical regimen.

Margaret (Mollie) Frederiksen majored in dance with a premed minor in biology at Mount Holyoke College in South Hadley, Massachusetts. She put those two concentrations together and chose a career as a physical therapist. "Taking Scientific Foundations of Dance opened my eyes to the world of biomechanics and kinesiology, and knowing how the body works to achieve the beautiful lines and shapes of dance changed my relationship with my own body in dance," she writes on the Mount Holyoke website. "It is this knowledge that I think makes me a better medical professional."

FROM FOOTWORK TO WORKOUTS

Sandy Tillett of New York City used her experience in dance performance to develop a career as a **Pilates/** exercise instructor. Like many who get into the dance field, her interest started as a young girl growing up in Elizabeth City, North Carolina. In time, she earned a bachelor of fine arts (BFA) degree in performance with a concentration in jazz dance from the University of North Carolina. She wound up working a lot with Troika Ranch, a New York City–based performance ensemble that incorporates body movement and technology. She would wear sensors on her body that might control video, sound, or lights.

To make ends meet as a dancer, she also worked part-time as a restaurant hostess and a personal trainer/exercise instructor. She started by working with three older women who wanted to stay in shape and stay active. She enjoyed teaching them movement and balance exercises. In time, she added more clients and shifted totally away from dance. She became a certified personal trainer and Pilates instructor.

"I've built a career out of it," Tillett says. "My favorite thing about dance is being in the rehearsal process. I like figuring things out. I like the interaction with a small group. One thing I realized about being a trainer is that I can get that. I can get all of the things I loved from the rehearsal process in a training environment. I like working one-on-one with my clients. There is a great exchange of ideas and a problem-solving element, like in a dance rehearsal process. If my clients can't do an exercise, we're going to figure out how we can make it work, even if it is modified. I like that. It's the same feeling I had in rehearsal."

Tillett adds that dancers are great at hands-on work because they are comfortable giving manual support. She has clients with multiple sclerosis who can't walk well—she will lift them and move their bodies. Because she has dance training, she feels she is finely tuned in to others' bodies and can help those who are having difficulties with motion. She plans on getting certification to teach the Feldenkrais Method, a system of movement, balance, and flexibility, and she continues to take Pilates classes herself. "As a dancer, class is so important. It's part of the process. And that's what I like about the work I'm doing now—I'm always going to be a student. I'm always learning and always evolving."

Dancing in a musical theater production is hard work, but it's also incredibly fun.

Getting involved with dance in school theater and other productions can lead to many rewarding experiences and may even shape a person's future career path (even if they don't get into dance). So consider giving dancing a try. Remember this as well: dancing is fun. As the writer Vicki Baum once said, "There are short-cuts to happiness, and dancing is one of them."

GLOSSARY

ad lib To perform, act, or speak before an audience without preparing or by going off script.

adrenaline A hormone released by the body's adrenal glands, especially during a time of stress. The hormone allows more blood to get to the muscles and more oxygen to get to the lungs quickly so physical performance can improve.

alignment Positioning of a specific body part with respect to the rest of the body. Usually refers to having the entire body in a perfect vertical posture from head to toes—the back is straight, abdominal muscles are pulled inward and upward, shoulders are down and relaxed.

audition A theatrical tryout; a test performance to get a role in a play, movie, television show, or other form of entertainment.

callback An invitation to return for a second audition.

characterization Developing a role into a character; giving a distinctive voice, language, look, and movement to the character.

conservatory A school in which students are taught music, theater, or dance.

core stability The ability of the muscles in the torso (such as abdominal and lower-back muscles) to maintain good posture and balance, especially during movement.

cross-training The action or practice of engaging in two or more types of exercise in order to improve fitness or performance.

cue Anything said or done, on or off stage, that signals a specific line or action to follow. For example, a door slam may be the cue for an actor to enter, or an actor's line may be the cue for the lights to change.

curtain call Taking a bow in front of the audience at the end of the show.

dialogue Conversation between two or more people in a play, movie, or other type of show.

double A person who substitutes for an actor in a scene, often to perform a difficult physical action or stunt; also called a "body double."

Feldenkrais Method A type of exercise therapy devised by Moshé Feldenkrais to reorganize connections between the brain and body, improving body movement and psychological state.

flamenco A style of spirited, rhythmic Spanish dancing and singing, characterized by hand clapping and foot stomping.

Gyrotonic movement Originally called yoga for dancers, an exercise regimen that emphasizes continuous, flowing movements, synchronized with corresponding breathing patterns.

improvisation A performance that is unplanned, unscripted, and spontaneously created by the performers.

lengthening Stretching exercises to extend leg muscles.

leotard A skintight, one-piece outfit made from stretchy fabric that covers the body from shoulders to upper thighs and is worn by dancers or people exercising indoors.

off book Performing the script from memory rather than reading it.

Pilates A system of exercises to improve physical strength, flexibility, posture, and mental awareness.

pointe work Ballet performed on the tips of the toes.

sight lines The line that runs from a seat in the audience to the stage, establishing the ease with which people can view a performance.

Somatic exercise Gentle movement patterns intended to shift the central nervous system to create new muscular habits.

sync To get people or things to move together in a harmonious way.

tech rehearsal A cue-to-cue rehearsal that focuses on the technical aspects of a production, such as light and sound.

tendinitis Inflammation of a tendon, which can lead to debilitating pain.

turnout Rotation of a dancer's legs from the hips, causing the knees and feet to turn outward.

understudy A performer who learns another's role in order to be able to replace that person on short notice.

FOR MORE INFORMATION

Books

Harris, Diana Dart. *Beginning Musical Theatre Dance.* Champaign, IL: Human Kinetics, 2016.

Joosten, Michael. *Dance and Choreography.* High School Musicals. New York: Rosen Publishing Group, 2010.

Lerch, Louise. *Broadway for Teens (Songbook): Young Women's Edition.* Milwaukee, WI: Hal Leonard, 2005.

Marsico, Katie. *Choreographer.* Cool Arts Careers. Ann Arbor, MI: Cherry Lake Publishing, 2012.

Schumacher, Thomas, and Jeff Kurtti. *How Does the Show Go On?: An Introduction to the Theater.* New York: Disney Editions, 2007.

Websites

Educational Theatre Association
https://www.schooltheatre.org/home
News, job listings, an events calendar, and other
resources aimed to help student theater groups.

The Guide to Musical Theater
http://www.guidetomusicaltheatre.com
This site provides a comprehensive list of links
to information of interest for those who love
musical theater.

Musicals101.com
http://www.musicals101.com
The "Cyber Encyclopedia of Musical Theatre, Film,
and Television" provides a long list of links to stories
on shows and performers, as well as to reviews, blogs,
and other reference materials.

Videos

Broadway or Bust
http://www.pbs.org/show/broadway-or-bust
Watch episodes of this PBS series from 2012 about
top high school musical performers in a competition
to see who is the best.

PS Dance!
http://psdancenyc.com
Paula Zahn with filmmakers Jody Gottfried Arnhold
and Nel Shelby created this Emmy-nominated
documentary that captures what happens when

students have dance in their curriculum. The film features Michael Kerr at Brooklyn's New Voices School of Academic & Creative Arts. You can get information about the documentary or watch it at this site.

DVDs

Berinstein, Dori. *Show Business: The Road to Broadway.* Dramatic Forces, 2007.

Kallis, Matthew. *Most Valuable Players.* Beverly Hills, CA: Canyonback Films, 2010. http://mostvaluableplayersmovie.com.

Price, Lonny. *Best Worst Thing That Ever Could Have Happened.* New York: Atlas Media Corp in association with Allright Productions, 2016. https://www.bestworstthingmovie.com.

INDEX

Page numbers in **boldface** are illustrations. Entries in **boldface** are glossary terms.

ABOUT THE AUTHOR

Don Rauf has written more than thirty nonfiction books, including *Music in Theater, Killer Lipstick and Other Spy Gadgets, Simple Rules for Card Games, Psychology of Serial Killers: Historical Serial Killers, The French and Indian War, The Rise and Fall of the Ottoman Empire*, and the book series *Freaky Phenomena*. He is a regular writer for Mental Floss and HealthDay. Don has loved musicals since grade school, when he performed in a production of *You're a Good Man, Charlie Brown*. He lives in Seattle with his wife, Monique, and son, Leo.